W9-BSU-243

Jimmy's Boa and the
Big Splash Birthday Bash

The residence of
MISS OLGA PEACHTREE
AND HER POODLE

Jimmy's Boa
and the
Big Splash Birthday Bash

by TRINKA HAKES NOBLE
pictures by STEVEN KELLOGG

Dial Books for Young Readers · New York

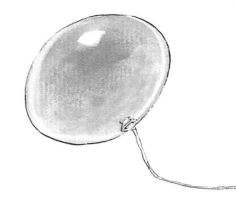

Published by Dial Books for Young Readers
A division of Penguin Young Readers Group
345 Hudson Street
New York, New York 10014

Text copyright © 1989 by Trinka Hakes Noble
Pictures copyright © 1989 by Steven Kellogg
Manufactured in China
Design adapted by Ann Finnell

E
9 10

Library of Congress Cataloging in Publication Data
Noble, Trinka Hakes.
Jimmy's boa and the big splash birthday bash/
by Trinka Hakes Noble; pictures by Steven Kellogg.
p.   cm.
Summary: Jimmy's birthday party at SeaLand turns out to be
a big splash when everyone ends up in the big tank.
ISBN 0-8037-0539-5.   ISBN 0-8037-0540-9 (lib. bdg.)
[1. Boa constrictor—Fiction. 2. Snakes as pets—Fiction.
3. Birthdays—Fiction.]
I. Kellogg, Steven, ill. II. Title.
PZ7.N6715Jh 1989 [E]—dc19 88-10933 CIP AC

The full-color artwork was prepared using ink and pencil line
and watercolor washes. It was then color-separated and reproduced
as red, blue, yellow, and black halftones.

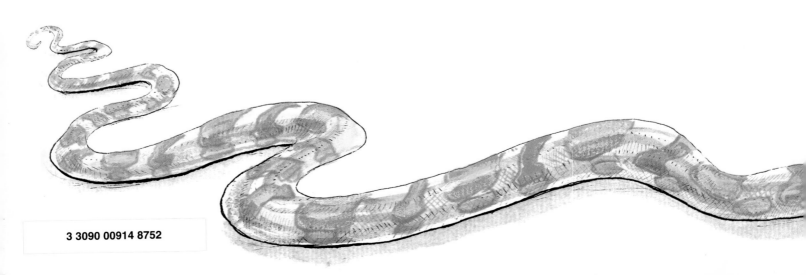

For Danny, Kathy, Jimmy, and Meghan, with love
T. H. N.

Love to dearest Emily
S. K.

Jimmy's
BIRTHDAY
PARTY
TODAY

"Hi, Meggie. How was Jimmy's birthday party at SeaLand?"
"Super...but a little soggy."

"Why, Meggie, you're soaking wet!"
"Well, it's not exactly dry inside a whale's mouth!"
"A whale's mouth? What were you doing inside a whale's mouth??"

"Trying to hide from the sharks."
"Sharks!! Sharks were chasing you?!?"

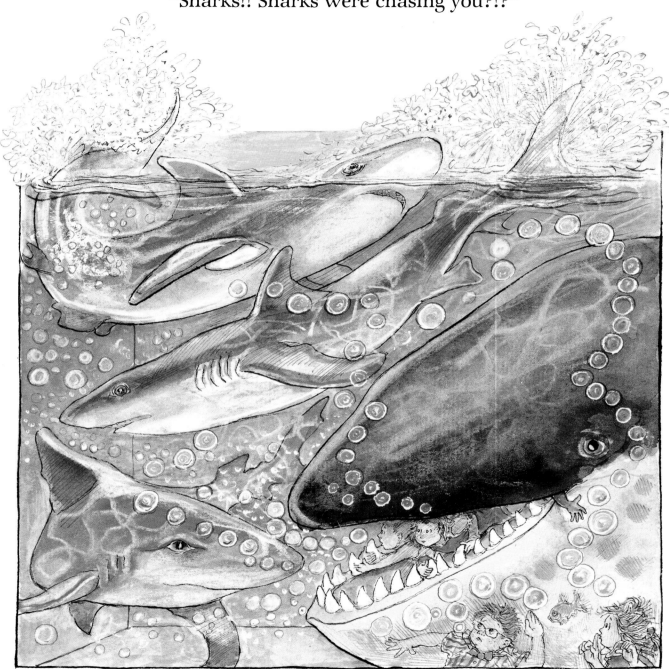

"Not really. We thought they were after Jimmy's new goldfish,
but Jimmy's pet boa constrictor saved it."

"Oh, no, that boa again! And now a goldfish?"
"Yeah, your friend Miss Peachtree caught the boa eating her
  laundry. He arrived just in time for the party, and the goldfish
  was a present from Jimmy's mom. She said it would make
  a nice, quiet, sensible pet. Boy, was she wrong!"

"She was?"

"Yeah, because Jimmy brought his new goldfish to SeaLand.
He wants to grow up to be a whale."
"Jimmy?"

"No, the goldfish. Anyway, Jimmy set his goldfish on the railing
of the big tank so he could see the whale.

"But when the whale came swooping up to give the trainer a kiss...it missed and kissed Jimmy's mom instead."

"It did?"

"Yeah, and it must have been a whale of a kiss because it knocked her and the goldfish bowl right into the big tank. Then all of us dove in."

"What?? You all dove into the big tank?"

"Yeah, as Jimmy's mom went flying over the railing, she yelled
'Dive right in,' so we did."
"But Jimmy's mom wouldn't yell that!"

"You're right, Mom. We thought she yelled 'Dive right in,' but she really yelled...

"'I CAN'T SWIM!!!!'"
"Oh, no! Did she get out all right?"

"Eventually. But we were too busy to help her. We had to catch Jimmy's goldfish before the sharks got it."

"Oh, and that's when you hid in the whale's mouth?"
"Right. And Jimmy's boa coiled himself around the shark's
    mouth to help us save the goldfish, but the sharks
    weren't really after it."
"They weren't?"

"No. These pushy seals kept bumping into them."
"Pushy seals?"

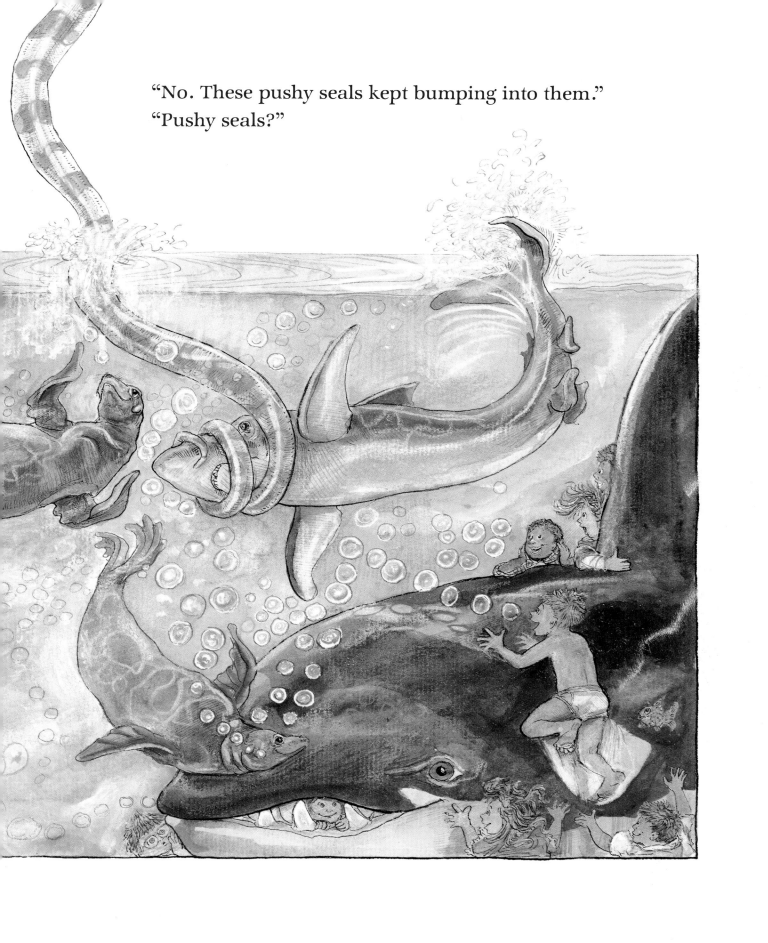

"Yeah, they were having this wild game of keep-away with Jimmy's goldfish bowl. I played on the penguins' side."
"There were penguins in the big tank?"

"Not really. The big tank was getting crowded and the sharks were getting mad, so we all went over to the penguins' tank."
"What? How did you get into the penguins' tank?"

"Well, Jimmy's boa made himself into a waterslide. So we all slid over to the penguins' tank to continue the game. That's why I smell this way."

"I wondered about that smell but was afraid to ask."

"Anyway, Mom, it was a great game between the penguins and the
seals until the trainer yelled and fished us out with a big net."
"Was the trainer mad?"
"No, he just told us that the party was over and to take a hike."

"But what about Jimmy's mom? Did the trainer pull her out too?"
"No, the net wasn't long enough. But Jimmy's boa reached down
   with his long tail and pulled her out.

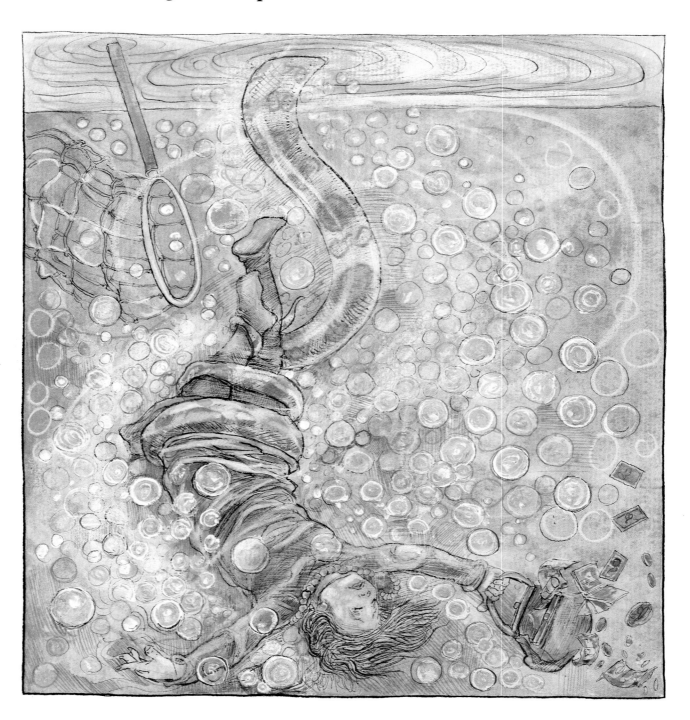

"That's the first time I ever saw her hug Jimmy's boa!"

"I bet Jimmy's mom was glad to get in the car and come home."

"Well, we didn't leave right away. Jimmy refused to go without his goldfish and bowl. When the trainer fished out the bowl, there was an octopus stuck in it. The trainer said we could keep the octopus if we'd just leave. So we did."

"What happened to the goldfish?"
"Oh, he stayed to become part of the whale's act, and that's why I need my allowance."

"Your allowance?"

"Yeah, since Jimmy lost his birthday present, we're all buying
him as many goldfish as we can. Bye."
"Wait!! Meggie…I'm not sure that's such a good idea….

"Oh, dear, I'd better phone Jimmy's mom."

"Thanks, Mom! That was the best birthday I ever had!"